By Mike Redston
& Bob Compton

Published in the UK by the BC Partnership Limited, One Eleven Edmund Street, Birmingham, B3 2HJ

Orders: Contact details can be found on the ARC Benefits Limited website www.arcbenefits.co.uk

Design: johnwatsondesign.co.uk

ISBN: 978-0-9566248-0-2

First Edition: March 2011

Printed in the United Kingdom

Effective observations on Pension Scheme Management

This book looks at an issue which is at the heart of every Company's pension scheme – the role that the Pensions Manager plays in the efficient delivery of pension benefits. Drawing on the substantial practical experience of the authors, the book provides useful insights to facilitate successful communication between trustees, scheme agents and company executives to improve management and raise standards.

Through utilising over 30 years of experience of both authors at the leading edge of pension scheme design and management, the book highlights aspects of Pension Scheme Management that the Company Board or Board of Trustees often rarely see and shows how the Pensions Managers' questions, instructions and statements can support and enhance the management process. It highlights the central influence of the Pensions Managers' role in binding effectively together all the key functions that must come together to have an efficient and beneficial pension scheme through insightful governance, policies and protocols.

This innovative book provides ideas, techniques and practical suggestions for delivering effective pensions management. It is key reading for Trustees, Pensions Managers, and Company Boards who are interested in improving the value to the Company of every pound of benefit paid out to members.

OVER REGULATED AND UNDER MANAGED?

UK Statutory Instruments & Regulations
affecting occupational pensions provision over 100 years

Period	Number	%
1910-69	5	0.5
1970-79	16	1.5
1980-89	100	9.6
1990-99	245	23.4
2000-09	680	65.0

Source: (Perspective)

UK pension schemes by Status
Sample: 6,596 defined benefit and hybrid schemes

Percentage of Schemes	2006 (%)	2010 (%)
Open	43	18
Closed to new entrants	44	58
Closed to new accrual	12	21
Winding up	1	2

Source: The Purple Book 2010

Facts:

1. In 100 years the UK has produced over 1000 regulations affecting pensions' provision.
2. Only 2% of regulations were published in the first 70 years.
3. The last decade produced 65% of all pensions regulations published over the last century!
4. The last decade introduced over 5 new sets of regulations on average for every single month!
5. The number of open UK pension schemes has dropped by 40% in the last 5 years!
6. More than 4 out of 5 UK pension schemes are now closed, compared to less than 3 out of 5, five years ago!
7. The Default Retirement Age is abolished in 2011.
8. Compulsory auto enrolment into Occupational Pensions commences in 2012 and will apply to all employers by October 2016.
9. The UK Pensions Regulator can issue fines of up to £5000 for individuals and £50000 for Companies, per failure to comply.
10. The UK Pensions Regulator has draconian powers of search.

How can the average Employer, Trustee or Pensions Manager hope to understand their respective obligations in the face of such change?

The following is an extract of a statement by the Pensions Regulator to scheme trustees issued in November 2009 titled "Good governance – keeping pensions safe".

"All those involved in pension schemes must bring examples of poor governance to our attention. There is a statutory requirement to whistleblow breaches of the law."

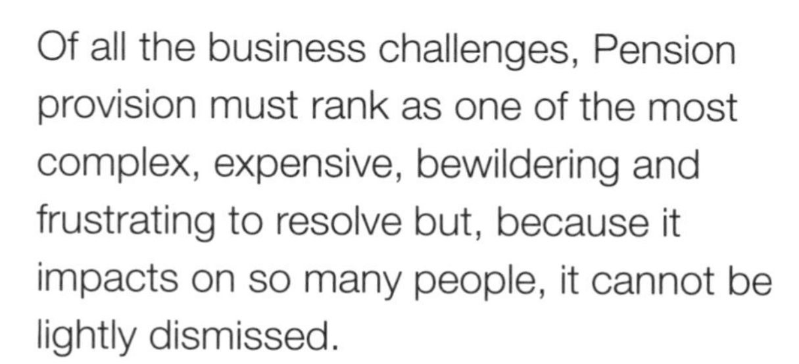

Of all the business challenges, Pension provision must rank as one of the most complex, expensive, bewildering and frustrating to resolve but, because it impacts on so many people, it cannot be lightly dismissed.

- 518 new UK regulations in 6 years to the end of 2010 demanding compliance
- Uneasy conflicts imposing themselves on Trustees and Employers
- Specialist technical issues blurring the bigger picture

Whatever your involvement in pensions, whether full or part time, we understand the range of problems being encountered, and the challenge confronting those with Pensions Management responsibility to keep everything hanging together and all the gaps plugged.

More than 30 years of practical pensions management experience have been distilled into our 108 ½ tips to help you regain control of the 'beastie' and prevent it from eating away at your resources, gnawing away at your sanity, stabbing you in the back, biting off your hand, or consuming your Company.

We hope that you will find this book a useful aid to:-

- save time and money
- understand the issues
- reduce conflicts and worry
- improve co-ordination and control

"All quotations inside this book are fictitious to protect the innocent and guilty"

With their parallel experiences of running a pensions department from the inside and advising a diverse range of businesses and trustees from the outside, Mike and Bob combine to produce a wide ranging knowledge of the many aspects involved in pension provision and how best to effectively link these all together. Both have been frustrated by the changed perception of pension provision over the last 30 years from a golden benefit to a heavy millstone. The move to outsource skills over the last 10 years and reams of new regulations have led Company Boards to grossly underestimate the need for effective management controls and an undervaluing of the role of the person with responsibility for managing the Pension Scheme. We felt it was now time to change that.

This book has been produced to provide an overview of the tasks traditionally undertaken by the Pensions Manager. As the role has become sidelined to a degree and other Company Executives take responsibility for their schemes as a part of a larger role, the book provides an overview of the nature of the task that is often overlooked and hence undervalued. But, particularly for organisations with defined benefit scheme deficits, the effective management of the scheme is crucial.

Hopefully this tips book will throw some light on what can be a debilitating challenge.

CONTENTS

100
TIPS TO TAME YOUR
'PENSIONS
BEASTIE'

1. A COMMON PURPOSE

Somebody once said:-
"The aim of all involved is to run the pension scheme as efficiently and cost effectively as possible"

Somebody else once thought:-
"We can make more money out of this if we take our time"

Someone else once proposed:-
"I'm prepared to agree reduced service levels if it saves money"

1. Ask those you are dealing with if they agree with the first statement

If not, ascertain their alternative or additional objectives so you know where you stand.

2. Concentrate on the important

Politely prevent others from wasting your or their time on matters of least impact.

3. Identify and work to the priorities

....but be conscious that ignoring someone else's priorities may create more disruption and effort in the long term.

4. Clarify and agree the policies and principles before tackling the detail

Encourage all involved to adopt this principle to avoid time wasting, expense and misunderstandings. Policies are there for a purpose so should be clear and work in practice.

5. Involve the right people at the right time

Involving the wrong people or organisations can be expensive and time consuming. By-passing the correct people or failure to reliably inform them creates inefficiency and pressure.

6. Distinguish between objectives, facts, opinions, interpretations and judgements

Differences of opinion and debates about interpretation can waste time, so start with facts and make sensible judgements based on these.

Accept legitimate facts without contention.

Unreliable information presented as fact is dangerous. Be aware of information that is unreliable or when an answer is unknown.

Opinions presented as fact are dangerous. To make progress, different opinions need harnessing in a common direction as quickly as possible.

Interpretations can be corrosive if misused to slant into a preferred direction or create doubts unproductively. Interpretations are a consequence of inaccurate facts, ambiguous wording or imprecise situations. Be wary of Interpretations.

Legal judgements are binding but not the quickest of methods to solve problems - far better to make sensible judgements earlier to prevent matters getting to these levels.

"It is my judgement that we should ask for a fifth opinion about the third interpretation of those facts. What do you think?"

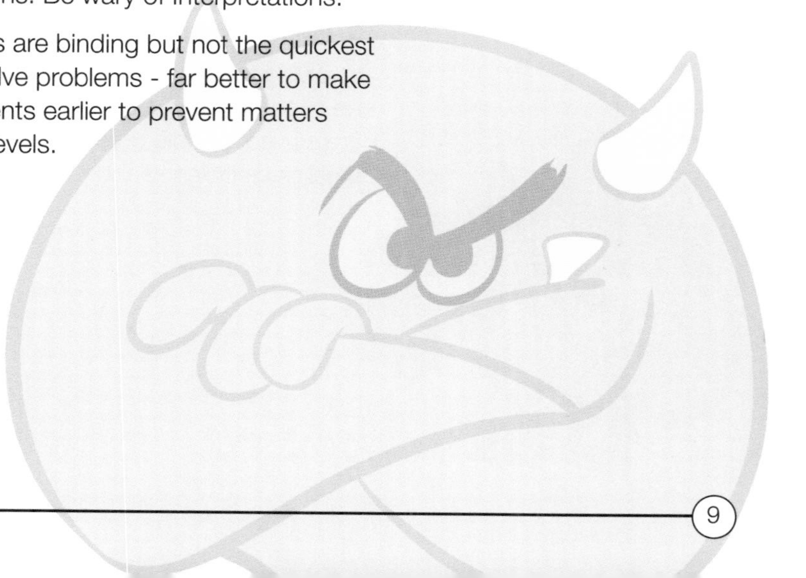

2. PENSION SCHEMES AND VOIDS

A former employee once said:-

"I've been in various schemes over 30 years but I don't know which"

.....in other words

"I'm not really interested whose problem it is - sort it for me"

7. Consider whose problem this is

This quotation is an example of a 'void' – a problem but whose? It may be the responsibility of a set of trustees or a particular employer or several but which?

8. Start by defining what you know

Identify your known pension scheme or schemes.

9. Locate and keep permanently accessible the legal documents establishing the scheme

Each scheme is unique and the constitutional documents (usually Trust Deeds and Rules) are the foundation of all that follows.

10. Research and record the origins and background

Pension schemes are based on history. Capture this history whilst you can from those who know.

Don't try to change or interpret history. Record history relevant for the future. Don't waste time on history which is of little relevance.

Identify the extent to which older schemes have been consolidated into replacements and any historical schemes that are still open and holding benefits.

11. Keep your Trust Deed and Rules up to date

Agree the principles of what is changing, what is being consolidated and what is not being consolidated.

To avoid getting out of control, agree in advance which parties are to be involved in the process. Agree the purpose and order of their involvement.

Ensure retention and easy access to older documents that have not been superseded by updates.

"I think the Company secretary deals with this; ask him"

12. Falling between stools: Think "Void"

There may be uncertainty as to who should do what or confusion on responsibility. There may be an easy and practical answer to the simple 'void' we started with, but other voids may be less obvious.

Aim to avoid the voids.

Constitutional documents define how to deal with the specifically known pension schemes. Progress onwards from these documents as a starting point.

Trustees are not empowered to deal with matters outside their defined remit, so there may be other significant 'voids' that someone else or some other body will need to deal with. Start by listing these and identifying responsibility. Then follow through appropriately.

Possible examples of these are: forgotten historical schemes that still exist; separate life assurance arrangements for non joiners; overseas worker deals.

3. POWERS, RESPONSIBILITIES, DECISIONS AND DELEGATION

A new Chief Executive boldly declared:-
"I've decided to discontinue the scheme"

A trustee once stated:-
"My purpose is to look after the interests of my work colleagues"

A trustee once said:-
"The process is more important than the outcome"

Another provocative thought:-
"I am unhappy with this decision but at least I've covered my back if it all goes pear- shaped"

13. Make sure those involved work within their powers

Although a statement of personal intent is a clear objective, **one** person on their own cannot make a definitive top level decision.

Make decisions as defined in the pension scheme's formal documents. Some may be exclusively down to the Trustees, others the Principal Employer and others a combination of both.

Ensure those involved know what their respective powers are.

14. Summarise the powers and make this summary easily available

Set out the powers summary in an easily understandable format. Powers that are understood will be accepted and followed.

Each party should acknowledge that others have responsibilities and understand their respective powers.

15. Make sure decisions are agreed by a correctly constituted quorum

This applies to both Trustee and Employer decisions. Be clear on the minimum number of people attending the meeting or passing a resolution as specifically required for the particular Company or Trustee body to be quorate.

Understand when a Chairman may give a casting vote. When exercised, clear minutes avoid future doubt.

Be clear when to seek approval at a higher level in the case of multi – tiered organisations. Again, minute formally to avoid doubt.

Ensure important decisions are clearly recorded and easily identifiable to avoid revisiting the same issues unnecessarily at a future date.

16. Delegate appropriately

Scheme documents may permit full delegation in certain circumstances.

Those with delegated authority may be empowered to make decisions and take action without further reference, or they may not.

Have a clear delegation policy.

Ensure the limits of power are clearly understood by both parties.

If in doubt, ensure that any decisions made at lower levels are formally recorded and approved.

Accept that delegation is essential for efficiency, but ensure controls are in place to prove delegated tasks are being undertaken reliably.

Regulations in the UK now require appropriate controls to be in place.

“A Chess board consists of a square, subdivided into a series of smaller squares that are all neatly defined. The challenge comes when you start moving pieces between the small squares and out of the big square. To win, you need to understand the Rules and implement a strategy. Managing a Pension Scheme is akin to a game of Chess except a Pension Scheme is not meant to be a contest.”

17. Understand the powers to appoint agents and apply these powers correctly

Some appointments are legally required and must be put in place. Some agents will be required to deliver defined and measurable end results; others may be consultancy-based, with varying degrees of subjectivity and pro-activity.

Be clear on Agents' responsibilities.

Ensure agents work to their obligations, within their powers and report reliably.

18. Take advice appropriately but avoid the tail wagging the dog

Advisers are not decision makers unless specifically required within their contractual obligations.

4. CUSTOMERS

19. Ensure all parties accept the need to serve

Efficient pension delivery relies on the co-operation of many parties, all serving and being served.

Ensure those at senior levels serve by giving clear information and guidance. Equally, they are served by receiving back good responses and evidence of efficient practices.

Trustees, Pensions departments, HR departments, Payroll departments, Accounts departments and External agents alike will all serve each other in different ways.

The ultimate end customers are the employees and members. Ensure they too play their part by providing reliable information about themselves very early in the process.

20. Serve as you would like to be served

Easier said than done! Good communication is one of the essential elements all the way up and down the line and into branch lines.

A king once proclaimed:
"You are my servants - I am your slave"

A negative thought:
"Not is the most dangerous word in the English Language; inaccurate omission or inclusion can have disastrous consequences."

5. EMPLOYERS

A Finance Director once confided:-

"I don't think the Parent Company understands the full implications of this. Do you think I should tell them?"

21. Identify the role of the Employer

Some schemes may no longer have any Employer involvement. Be clear whether this is, or is not, the case.

22. Understand the Organisational Structure of the Employer

This may vary from a single Limited Company to a very complex ever-changing group. With business acquisitions and sales and name changes, ensure that the correct legal entities are involved at principal and participating level.

23. Understand the people

Put yourself in their shoes and consider not only their personalities but their different perspectives. Consider the differences in perspective of the following:

- Chief Executive of overseas parent Company;
- Chairman and major shareholder;
- Non executive Director on many plc Boards;
- Company Secretary;
- Finance Director of a sub division;
- Chairman of a Remuneration Committee;
- Financial Controller who is also a trustee;
- Small Business Owner.

These examples are at senior levels with potentially different angles of approach.

Careful handling that harnesses these into a common direction will avoid time wasting and cost. Be aware that similar dilemmas may arise deeper down within organisations.

A muse:

"A Manager is either a person who copes, or a problem that ages men at a quicker rate than women."

24. Structure to suit the Organisation

In many ways, a simple one Company operation is the easiest to structure but can put pressure on senior employees or owners who want to concentrate on their main business rather than pensions.

Delegation to specialists is an obvious route but makes the organisation very vulnerable to over-dependency and increasing costs without suitable structures to give assurances that all is under control.

Another muse:

"A Womanager is either a device to bring female life expectancy in line with the males, or the next development of political correctness."

Ideally, for larger organisations, the pension management structure should be compatible with the main business organisational structure, but differences may need to be recognised.

Be clear where a pensions department or pension manager or person responsible for pensions sits in the context of the organisational structure to ensure efficiency through the whole range of pensions processes.

Controls should be in place regarding who, and at what levels, are empowered to engage directly with trustees or external service providers and under what circumstances.

5. EMPLOYERS (CONTINUED)

25. Beware of incompatible practices

Discrepancies in Employment contracts, inappropriate pension negotiations and failure or delay in following administrative procedures can result in unbudgeted expense and embarrassment.

26. Consider pensions as soon as possible in business changes

The value of pension benefits can exceed the value of a business so should not be an afterthought.

The topic can be very contentious and provocative.

A business sale, for example, could create four separate stances - the buyer, the seller and 2 sets of trustees, who may have no obligation to abide by a business agreement signed by Employers.

For various reasons the Pensions Regulator may become involved.

Crystallise principles early to minimise spiralling agent costs and, if possible, establish a defined process for managing such events in a controlled way.

6. TRUSTEES

27. Be clear of the trustee constitution and methodology of appointment

Whether a Trustee Company or individual trustees, whether selected, nominated or elected, whether a member or an independent, appointments must be dealt with correctly. Check against the powers and set out how these are dealt with. Specify clear terms of tenure and responsibility (and payment if applicable).

Plan to ensure continuity and stability in the event of unexpected changes or absences.

28. Specify expectations and special roles

Much time wasting, soul searching and expense can be substantially reduced by clarifying:

- what individual trustees are expected to do themselves outside of routine meetings,
- the terms of reference of any working groups or sub committees and
- the roles of Chairman, Secretary or any other specialist roles.

Be clear regarding relationships with agents (including pension manager or pensions department) to avoid duplication, omission or lack of control and unexpected costs.

Ever had these thoughts in a meeting?

Why am I here?

Why is he here?

Who's running this meeting?

What am I supposed to do with these documents?

> "A journey may comprise of a number of transport changes. A change in the scheduled time of one of these may prevent you reaching your destination."

29. Plan timetables, routines and Meetings

Many activities are repetitious within regular cycles, enabling a well organised approach to be adopted; meetings should be planned around these with good advanced notice, attendees and reports appropriate to the topic and efficient follow up activity.

Where an employer is still relevant, it is sensible to include meetings with the Employer in the process.

In the same way as the Employer is likely to require periodic reports from the trustees or pensions manager, it is not inappropriate for the trustees to request a routine Employer report.

30. Deserve the Trust

Vested interests and biases have no place. The trustee body as a whole is to be 'trusted' by members, employers and other parties to carry out a unified purpose.

There will be access to confidential information which is to be respected.

7. AGENTS

31. Appoint external agents sensibly

Some agents have to be appointed by law; make these appointments as required. Thereafter, determine what is expected to be done internally and make sensible appointments for the remainder of the work in accordance with the powers of appointment.

Be clear which are of an ongoing nature and which for one off activities and construct the agreements appropriately.

Have clear balanced agreements – a totally one sided agreement is not a good agreement – and clearly defined service requirements and expectations.

Understand the powers of sub-contracting and responsibilities where sub-contracted. Monitor services against the standards set.

Be clear who the agent is accountable to (Trustee, Employer or both).

A consultant stated:

"I know more about your scheme than you do...leave it to me"

An Investment Manager thinking about an Investment Adviser:

"He's never done any investment himself so hasn't a clue...but he puts a lot of business our way"

32. Keep agents under control

Regular reporting and monitoring against benchmarks and standards should be automatic.

Methodologies should be in place for reporting exceptions/errors.

Be clear who the agent is meant to report to and what methodology is in place for authorising and paying for time cost or extra work falling outside of the scope of known fees.

The reciprocal thoughts of the Investment adviser:

"He's very good at what he does but he doesn't understand the bigger picture at all"

7. AGENTS (CONTINUED)

"In 1970, pensions lawyers were a rare breed usually found tucked away in the family trusts department. Today in every large practice there is a pension law department and there are specialist practices that concentrate solely on pension law. A whole new generation of Lawyers has been created."

"Similarly over the last two decades Actuaries have had to transform from back room number crunchers to front line problem solvers."

"Some might argue these structural changes are at the root of the current problems."

Ensure all projects are managed to minimise the potential for running out of control and that any direct dealings between agents are authorised and known about.

Where possible, agree in advance when it is necessary to have agents acting separately for the Trustees and the Employer, and the scope of their roles and timing of involvement.

Ensure a proportionate balance between time and quality.

33. Make changes logically and justifiably

Some changes may be strategically driven, others through dissatisfaction with the service provided. Whatever the reason, recognise the risks involved in disruption and agree a mechanism for the smoothest possible transition.

Try to minimise the period of uncertainty but be realistic on timescales. Remember that newly appointed agents, however good, will know less about your scheme than an outgoing agent, however bad; try to maintain the good-will of the outgoing agent.

Debrief the outgoing agent. Be clear on where the division of responsibilities lies between the old and new agent, and what rests elsewhere.

Some changes may require rapid action. Involve the right people quickly, identify who is to manage the change and get on with it.

34. Remember that experts in their specialist areas are not automatically experts on your scheme and its circumstances

There are two aspects to this:-

First ensuring sufficient internal knowledge and having information readily available.

Second, minimising the time and expense incurred (at your expense) of the agent finding out what should already be available.

Agents may deal with many schemes and clients, and human nature can confuse one with the other on occasions.

8. KNOWLEDGE AND UNDERSTANDING

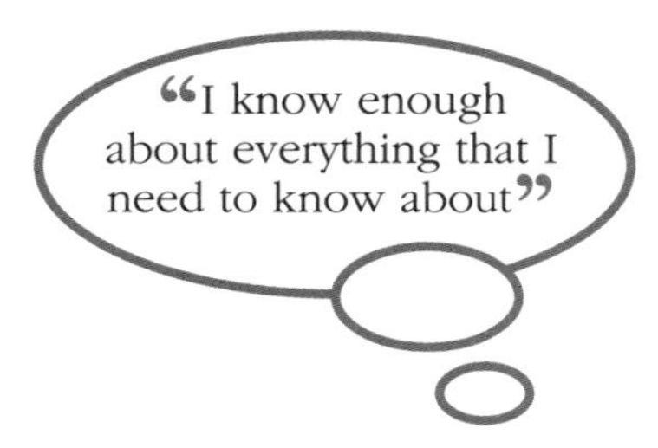

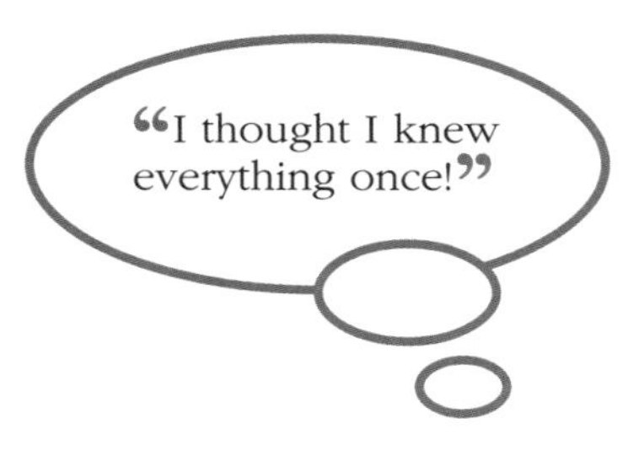

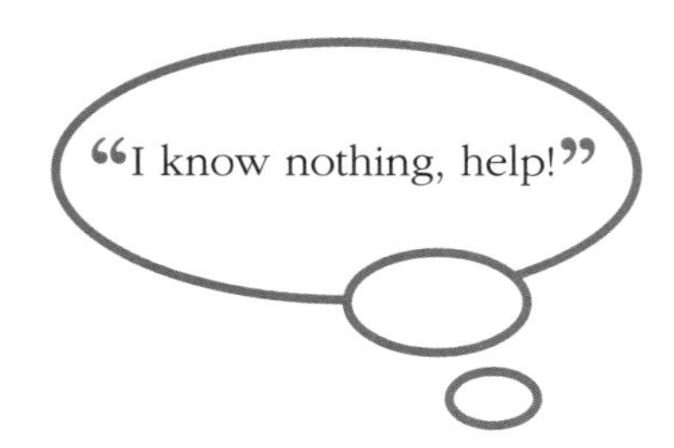

35. Aim for continuity and combined knowledge

People can leave and move on unpredictably; do not undervalue the advantages of combined knowledge – a well trained individual is of no value if no longer available.

Trustees are expected to have training in line with Regulator guidance. Implement a programme and keep training records that are easily accessible.

Trustees are given immediate powers on appointment. Put in place a mechanism for providing key information easily and quickly for stability and continuity purposes.

Apply these principles to others involved in the pension chain.

36. Distinguish between functionality and decision making

Whether a trustee, an employee or an external agent, those carrying out functional roles need to know what they have to do, how to do it and when they have to refer and report.

However knowledgeable about their subject in general, ensure the requirements specific to your scheme are readily available in an easily understandable format.

Decision makers need to understand enough to make sensible decisions and need to recognise any practical implications, but should not be expected to understand intricate specialist detail.

37. Acknowledge the knowledge gaps

No-one should be afraid to admit to not knowing or of asking 'stupid questions' but over-zealous or time wasting diversions need to be put in context of other priorities.

Controlled training and information provision can reduce distractions.

Be wary of training for training's sake alone.

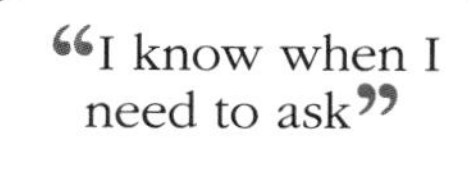

9. BENEFIT DESIGN

"I know my rights."

"I was planning to retire at 60 but now you say I can't."

"I know we are not married but we've been living together for 22 years."

"HR said that I'd get extra pension if I accepted redundancy."

38. Make guarantees the priority

For a Defined Contribution Scheme, the promise is the amount of money going in. Ensure delivery of the promise is not compromised by delayed or unreliable contribution payments.

Life Assurance may be an additional promise but may be subject to underwriting or other conditions. Ensure these are carried out reliably and premiums paid appropriately.

Defined Benefit Schemes are more complex,

- the pensions promise is based on a formula payable from a normal retirement age;
- details and precise definitions will be scheme specific;
- additional benefits such as death benefits, pension increases are provided;
- options for cash and early retirement may be available with varying degrees of complexity.

Be clear - is the benefit an entitlement, or subject to the exercise of discretion?

Whilst it has to be recognised that cast iron guarantees are virtually impossible, the priority should be to protect the rights earned in the past.

Ensure any life assurance risks, if these are still promised, are covered.

39. Be clear about the discretions, practices and other potential obligations

These may fall into a number of categories. Some of these will clearly need consideration on an individual basis.

For example:-

- ill health retirement enhancements,
- dependants' benefits upon death.

Clarify what may be rights and what may require the exercise of discretion and by whom.

Standard practises, e.g. early retirement: Is this a right, either within the scheme documents or possibly some other form of agreement with Unions or contractual with the employee in some way? If a right, is it a scheme obligation or does the Employer cover the additional cost?

Most early retirement factors are deemed broadly financially neutral, or perhaps there is a formula built into the design; whichever, be aware of the basis and cost implications?

Broadly financially neutral covers a multitude of sins. Is this on a cash equivalent transfer basis, going concern, wind up, average or member specific basis? Knowing the cost impact on the Fund, and ultimately the Employer, can ensure funding costs do not run out of control.

Distinguish between rights and concessions for Pension Increases. Who has the power to make these decisions and what are the implications?

Even if nothing changes, it is advisable to ensure that practices are endorsed from time to time or as required by any constitutional documentation. Record these for easy future reference.

A word of caution: check what communication goes out to members when giving quotations or notifications to ensure that discretions do not inadvertently become rights.

40. Take major changes very seriously

To coin a phrase: "don't fix it if it 'aint broke".

Employers, though, need to consider their costs and employment needs. Trustees must carry out their obligations. Liability reduction and benefit protection do not make comfortable bed-mates, so it is not an easy ride.

Sensible management and communication can smooth and simplify the path and avoid major confrontational overtures from the outset.

Although not fashionable in the current climate, and perhaps a provocative and nostalgic thought, but if the objectives are clear (including ensuring each party acts within their powers), how about asking one consultant or lawyer to find a solution satisfactory to both Trustees and Employer?

10. FINANCES

41. Unravel the layers of cost

Some are visible: what is actually paid and recorded. Others may be hidden (e.g. commission or investment trading costs) and others may be unquantifiable such as staff or director time spent on pensions. There may also be hidden savings like national insurance contributions or tax.

A dubious assumption:

"it's alright – the pension scheme pays"

42. Be clear who is commissioning work, who should pay and the mechanics of authorising and paying invoices

Pension schemes hold large sums of money. There can be a temptation or expectation that the fund will pay (either directly or as offsets or re-imbursement) regardless of value or necessity.

A frustrated financial director:-

"Nothing irks me more than being summoned to a meeting with the Trustees and being confronted with vast teams of consultants, lawyers and hangers-on that I'm expected to pay for."

43. Plan

Trustees should prepare budgets, and control and understand the quantum of benefit payments and costs.

Include cash-flow planning, taking into account the relationship between anticipated benefit payments and available funds. Be clear where the cash is to come from and if required the disinvestment methodology and associated costs.

Apply a discipline on trustees costs (in a co-operative way); ultimately it is the Employer who has to foot the bills.

44. Ensure effective practices

Reconcile appropriate bank accounts. Monitor actual occurances against expectations. Receive reports and identify exceptions.

10. FINANCES (CONTINUED)

A disciplined approach will pick up errors earlier, often without causing irreparable damage.

Ensure processes are efficient and integrated. Contribution deductions, payments and onward payments, and incoming and outgoing payments should work like clockwork. Inefficient processes, because there are so many people involved, can take an unacceptably long time to transact accurately from start to finish.

45. Have clear Accounting practices and procedures

Formal annual accounts are required for the Pension Scheme and, if applicable, for a Trustee Company and are methodologies for crystallising and signing off historical information as accurate; statements about future expectations or subsequent events will also be included.

Similarly, Company Accounts need to accurately reflect pension information, including solvency levels and individual Director arrangements.

In addition, there are likely to be accounts at other times such as quarterly or monthly updates.

As the processes will require the involvement of a number of parties exchanging information, there is not an easy distinction between what may be a Trustee or an Employer responsibility or a pensions, accounts or secretarial departmental responsibility and the respective roles of actuaries and auditors acting for either the Trustee or Employer or both.

This is a complex area that without care can be muddied. The processes need to be clear and sensibly managed.

11. THREE KEY TOPICS

46. Stand back and think of the big picture

There is a simple view that by getting Administration, Funding and Investment right, all will run smoothly.

There is no doubt that all three are critically important but, before we look at the implications of each, consider their relative importance– what are the priorities?

There is no right answer of course! Each area deserves detailed attention. The three topics are covered next in no particular order of priority!

12. ADMINISTRATION

Said with patience on the phone:-

"You may be right 99% of the time but I am afraid I am in the 1% you got wrong and that was 100% wrong for me"

47. Try to define what is meant by Administration for your scheme

One dictionary definition says to 'administer' is to 'manage' so administration could be the whole realm of pensions management as required by Trustees and Employers and the law.

Be aware of what others mean when they talk about administration? There is a high possibility that it is not identical to your understanding.

There is a general acceptance that the Administrator appointed by the Trustee to do benefit calculations is the Administrator; what else does this administrator do – do they run the bank account, deal with the members directly, do the Regulator returns, organise the accounts, run the pensions payroll, draft the booklets etc.? What don't they do?

In other circumstances, the trustee body is regarded as the administrator i.e. they have administration responsibilities, and the statutory bodies expect there to be a named administrator for their purposes.

There are also pensions administrators at employer site level and in pensions departments and so it goes on.

48. Concentrate on the functionality

If you strip away anything requiring a decision or judgement or discretion, then administration may simply be represented as a requirement to carry out certain actions at certain times in a prescribed way.

Although perhaps soul-less and mechanistic, if this 'works like clockwork' at all operational levels then administration becomes efficient. Of course it can then be improved by personality and style but the fundamentals are in place.

Example links in the chain - carried out by different people - are recruitment, joining scheme, payroll deductions, contribution payments, data to scheme, salary changes, marriage, leaving, transfers, dying, divorce, retiring, quotations, benefit statements, payment of pensions.

However arduous to produce, setting out a clear process with comprehensible instructions in an administration manual, readily available to all involved should improve efficiency.

Preparing the manual will also highlight areas of weakness and inefficiency.

Plan for review and update the manual regularly. Include instructions for this process in the manual!

49. Don't ignore the need for the overview

The danger with computerised calculations and systemised approaches is that they may miss the obvious or accept the inaccurate as factually correct. The correct calculations need to be produced.

Instinctive overviews and checking to ensure answers are in line with expectations will help reduce errors of larger impact.

50. Have an open discussion about data reliability

If data is historically wrong, it may be impossible to prove what is or is not accurate.

A letter to pensioners:-

"Every now and then we have to check you still exist. Please confirm whether or not you are dead. If you do not reply within a month we will assume you are dead and suspend your pension."

A Pensioner's Reply:-

"Thank you for your interest in my well-being. I am sure you are aware that I am alive, as you've been sending me a pension each month. As I cannot guarantee to be able to inform you when I die, I am enclosing a sealed envelope notifying you to that effect. You are authorised to open it when that event occurs. When it does occur, please be careful where in space you suspend my pension, as I am not yet sure of my direction of travel."

With scheme changes and administrator changes, there is very often a data verification exercise undertaken; sometimes this is essential but on other occasions unnecessary if the data is already known to be robust.

In doing a valuation, an actuary may well make some allowances for potentially inaccurate data, sometimes rather arbitrarily. It would seem very sensible to clear the air on any data concerns in a non confrontational way.

This may be difficult if there are already strongly held views that a particular party may be potentially liable or if some form of insurance claim is being pursued. Whereas there may be financial or justifiable reasons to follow this latter route, it is unlikely to be the most efficient way of establishing reliable data.

Ensure confidentiality of data is protected at all levels and reliable back up procedures are in place.

Special exercises should be undertaken as appropriate for death verification, tracing missing beneficiaries etc.

51. Receive reports and identify the weak links and weaknesses

It is generally accepted that an administrator appointed by the Trustees will provide regular reports. These should be useful in identifying how efficient the administrator is and show membership information and changes. It should show where things are waiting responses from others (including where the administrator may be waiting for a trustee decision or more information from an employer).

An efficient administrator's reputation can be tarnished by delays from others, particularly if they are in the front line of complaints as a consequence, so efforts should be made to identify and deal with any inefficiency here.

The scheme administrator report can only show what is known, so, where employers are involved in the supply of information, reconcile with the payroll.

52. Don't forget member communication, time limits and complaints procedures

There are laid down disclosure requirements on what members must receive automatically or get on request, and stated time limits. Ensure there is a mechanism in place to know that these are being adhered to, where responsibility lies in drafting, printing and issuing, or alternative mechanisms like websites.

For standard communication like member quotations, benefit statements or payslips, check the extent to which these are or need to be specific to your own scheme's structure.

Do everything well and complaints will be rare, but ensure that any complaints are dealt with correctly in line with your procedure.

53. Adopt a timetable approach for other elements of administration

Whether responsible for accounts, regular communication, IT, investment, custody, provision of actuarial factors, payment of contribution or other pension related activities, the same logic should apply to administrative functions attached to them; identify and work to a planned timetable for the regular routines and obtain appropriate evidence that they have been carried out reliably.

13. INVESTMENT

"Investment Managers have a talent for spending other people's money.

The good ones are adept at spending it shrewdly.

The bad ones are adept at telling you they are adept at spending it shrewdly.

The difficult judgement is to know which is which before it's too late."

54. Understand the investment extremes and what options are in the middle

Lottery type gambling is clearly a non starter. At the other end of the spectrum, transferring risk by annuity purchases is receiving much attention. In the middle sit the other categories - equities, fixed interest, cash, property etc. with various specialist permutations.

55. Understand the types and styles of investment management approach

These include segregated, balanced, unitised and specialist funds with varying degrees of complexity.

56. Understand the support needs

These could include Investment Consultants, Actuaries, Investment Managers, Custodians, Banks, Accountants, Auditors, Investment Monitors, Transition Managers, Tax specialists etc. Different structures will place different demands on the above so this needs careful attention to control sensibly.

57. Consider the strategy in the right order

Although the Trustees will make the decision, they most certainly will require advice. The Employer has an interest, as it ultimately foots the bills but will also know more about certain aspects than the Trustees.

The start point is bringing together the pertinent facts or information, including the data profile, the strength of the Employers' Covenant, actuarial assumptions being made and any known potential significant events. The latter may well need sensitive and confidential handling, but all of these need sensible dialogue on how to construct the Trustees' 'Statement of Investment Principles' so that it is satisfactory to both parties and minimise the potential for conflict.

If the major top-level principles can be agreed, the Employer should then be able to stand back and trust the Trustees to develop the detail, reporting on developments as appropriate.

Place in order of severity:

Trickle;
flood;
drip;
torrent;
leak.

Select suitable reactions from the following:

Repair;
divert;
run away;
Swim; drink;
turn off tap;
build a dam;
panic; have a cup of tea;
plug the hole with your finger;
hire a boat;

58. Identify the Cash-flow impact

This will be specific to your scheme's circumstances and is not something a consultant can be expected to know without input. There may be a regular pattern which would help understand the extent to which disinvestment may or may not be required to cater for benefit payments. Additionally, anticipated exceptional events need factoring in to the strategy.

59. Identify acceptable levels of complexity

Scheme size may well dictate what investment structure can be tolerated and supported, i.e. how many managers and what type of manager, but Trustees also need to understand the administrative impact of any decisions.

There may be a well-supported strategic argument for appointing a particular manager, and this is likely to be the consultant's emphasis when putting forward recommendations for long lists and short lists etc. This will also be the Managers' emphasis when selling themselves, plus perhaps the efficiency of their own internal administrative procedures and reporting.

Consider the difference between these two:-

(i) An index-tracking, unitised (pooled) fund and

(ii) An overseas equity fund, segregated (i.e. specific for the scheme with its own investments) and multi layers of custodians, currency dealings, trading structures, transactions and tax treatment etc.

The first will generate very little administrative effort outside of the manager, possibly little more than one monthly statement that is not complex to reconcile.

The second could generate large quantities of form filling, transaction information, tax reclaims etc., with a knock-on effect to pensions departments, secretaries to Trustees, Trustees themselves, accountants, investment monitors, auditors, actuaries etc. demanding much more analysis and scrutiny and scheme ownership and responsibility.

Does the complexity of operation negate the perceived benefits?

60. Set the right benchmarks, monitor appropriately and understand the costs

At one time, the concept was very simple. All pension schemes were bundled together and success or failure rated by whether your scheme performed better or worse than anybody else's over say one, three or five year periods, with managers being praised for even shorter 3 monthly periods of achievement.

Performance related fees (the bonus culture) has come into sharp focus.

Specific scheme related strategies, targeted to the scheme profile, now place much more emphasis on specifically tailored benchmarks.

A correctly thought out benchmark should make it simpler to measure how well the managers do what they are being paid to do.

Be clear how fees and costs (direct or indirect) are reflected, within the benchmark measurement. Pre determine and record over what periods it is logical to make critical judgements.

61. Review regularly and manage changes sensibly

Performance and overall strategy need regular review.

Identify areas of risk.

Timing is critical in investment, but pensions are predominantly long term, so perhaps not always so critical, but judging when to change can be difficult.

Clearly identify who has responsibility to flag up areas of concern, particularly where these may need urgent action.

Any disinvestment or changes to an investment manager or investment profile have implications beyond the simple decision to change.

Clarity of responsibility for managing effective change is also needed to minimise any detrimental impact.

62. Spare a thought for the members

Decisions on investment strategy within a defined benefit scheme, and the management of these, ultimately have a major impact on the ability to successfully pay individual benefits in accordance with the formulae.

13. INVESTMENT (CONTINUED)

A well thought-out strategy could, through circumstance, disappoint; alternatively a bad strategy could, through luck, be surprisingly successful. There are no absolute rights or wrongs but a matter of applying sensible judgements on acceptable risks.

In Defined Contribution Schemes (including Additional Voluntary contributions), risk falls to the individual.

There can be a real dilemma on how much information or support is made available to members.

Draw a line between what the Trustees and the investment providers make available.

Be clear, where there are choices, how the individual makes their choice. Establish the extent of any guidance given by the Employer and whether independent advice should be provided as a facility or be purely down to the individual.

For Defined Contribution Schemes similar questions arise on conversion of the fund to benefit as to how to ensure best value. Whether a Trustee, member or Employer, the objective is the same – to get the best out of what is paid in.

Work together to find the best solution.

Develop an efficient conversion process from fund to annuity payment in the months leading up to Retirement. Undue delay can be experienced in establishing a member's pension if the process is effectively unmanaged.

14. FUNDING

63. Dream a dream (some might say now the impossible dream)

Think non technically to find a starting point and imagine the following: an average business, no pension fund deficit or surplus, trustees and employers with no particular axe to grind, a neutral actuary, investment portfolio and strategy in line with assumptions, no plans to change an efficiently run scheme and no legal reasons to change.

With reliable data input, acceptable answers would drop out, showing the pension contributions to be paid, additional amounts like PPF levy and life assurance costs, plus an allowance for expenses (modest because scheme well run).

Employers would then pay as required into the scheme, and thereafter the trustees would ensure efficient investment and administration and costs within budget. Easy, isn't it?

64. Don't panic about the Nightmare

The reverse would be challenging, with many parties crawling all over the problems, conflicts brewing and likely changes to personnel involved as efforts are made to re-structure. All very costly, confusing and disruptive.

Message: Think and act calmly; a way through can be found.

A PLAYLET:

NEVER MIND THE QUALITY,
GET THE DRIFT.

Chairman:
"I trust the actuary with my life."

Finance Director:
(in jocular fashion)
"Good job it wasn't your death; he expected you to die on your birthday last week."

(hearty laughter)

Chairman:
(tutting)
"That's mere detail. The detail is not important."

Accountant:
(opportunistically)
"Would you authorise this please."

(He passes papers to Chairman)

Chairman
(after a pause):
"...but that's 37p out!"

Accountant:
(rather too quickly)
"We always round to whole pounds."

Finance Director:
(in jocular fashion)
"He'd have signed it if you'd followed the Actuary's example and rounded to the nearest £100,000"

(hearty laughter)

Chairman:
(with authority and frowning)
"I expect accuracy!"

Accountant:
(tentatively and appealing to Financial Director for support):)
"..... but you did just say that you were not interested in detail and last week that I was a bit too pernickety."

Chairman
(educationally):
"It totally depends upon the circumstances. There is a time and place for everything and this is an occasion for d....."
(He drifts away and slumps in his chair)

65. Understand the Actuary's position

Rather uniquely and somewhat perversely, a scheme actuary is appointed as an individual not an organisation. In practice, he or she will need to rely on input from others and will be aware of the scope for negotiation, so may well be cautious in his approach.

There will be a range of assumptions that the Actuary may be prepared to consider but, because of personal accountability, there will be items where there is little or no scope for manoeuvre, whatever the pressures.

Equally, another actuary appointed by the Employer with a different perspective, and no personal accountability, may argue there is considerable scope.

66. Understand the Employers' position

Likely to acknowledge it has an obligation to fund the scheme but may well be uncomfortable with the magnitude and unknown nature of this.

Will naturally want to keep costs as low as possible. May be willing to consider input of extra money if some of the obligations and liabilities can be removed.

Will only be able to pay what the business can afford and will have other pressures from shareholders, owners etc.

May wish to consider all available options for liability reductions and take advice.

May well wish to use its own advisers independently of the trustees' advisers.

Will be conscious that the Employers ability to pay (Covenant) is a key aspect to what the Trustees need to consider and that the PPF levy is higher where this ability is suspect.

Will acknowledge that Trustees need information on this but will be cautious of releasing confidential information.

67. Understand the Trustees' position

Will be aiming to ensure as much funding as possible to support the benefit promises.

The more doubts about the Employers covenant (ability to pay), the more they would like before it's too late.

The more mature a scheme and weaker the covenant, the 'safer' the investment tends to become, reducing the optimism for investment growth and thus pushing up the costs of benefit provision.

68. Find the common ground

The Trustees have to produce both a Statement of Funding Principles and a Statement of Investment Principles. These need to be compatible. These should not be imposed upon the Employer in a cavalier fashion and require sensible discussion and ideally full agreement.

Break down the components into relevant areas of knowledge. For example, neither trustees nor employers nor their respective advisers can claim to know better answers to general economic conditions than anyone else, so finding common ground should not be contentious.

(General consternation)

Finance Director:
(with respectful jocularity)
"I assume he was going to say 'detail' and not 'death'. But look on the bright side - being only a week out is exceptionally good detail for an actuary."

(Curtain falls)

Rather disappointingly the drama critic was not too impressed with the quality of the playlet, or any of the figures - with the notable exception of the figure of Amelia, who played the non speaking role of the Secretary.

14. FUNDING (CONTINUED)

Scheme specific assumptions are then a matter of identifying how the scheme is likely to vary from these benchmarks and who may be the most knowledgeable about any particular items. For example, an Employer should know more about expected salary changes and leavers etc. than the Trustees or an actuary and should give responsible input.

Rates of pension increase may be purely linked to inflation or fixed, in which case the Actuary should easily be able to produce answers; but, if subject to discretion there is a need to identify who is best equipped to advise what is likely to happen/wanted into the future. If the formulae are complex, there is a similar need to identify who is best equipped to ensure the Actuary is suitably aware of the complexity.

Another element is Mortality (expectation of when people will die). It may be known that a particular industry or geographical location has better or worse experience than normal. It is also quite possible to obtain specific mortality knowledge about your own scheme's history and, for a large scheme, an influencing factor. Whether or not this is relevant to the future expectations is up for debate.

Buying annuities as an alternative to paying pensions from the scheme assets, is primarily an investment decision but it also has a risk reduction aspect.

If deaths in your scheme were historically at a younger age than normal what is the scope for the annuity cost to reflect this?

The issue for Actuary and Trustees and Employer to address together is what evidence (if any) is available on history and how relevant this is to the future.

Investment assumptions are a substantial topic depending upon levels of acceptable risk relevant to the scheme's profile, and involve having a correct relationship between the actuarial assumptions and the investment strategy and portfolio.

69. Understand the Pension Regulators position

Very simply, the Regulator wants all schemes to be funded sufficiently to provide the benefits and to avoid a burden falling on the Pension Protection Fund. It expects Trustees to act responsibly and Employers to honour their obligations (see Appendix 1).

The Regulator needs informing of certain significant events ('notifiable events') and can be asked to give clearance before certain actions are to be carried out.

The Regulator recognises that there are difficult challenges and is able to endorse specific funding plans constructed to solve difficulties.

The Regulator should be viewed as a friend capable of endorsing practice, rather than a menacing quango capable of inflicting great pain if disobeyed.

70. Understand what is meant by surplus or deficit

In defined benefit schemes, this is only crystallised at the point of closure. Prior to that, it is based on assumptions. In scheme actuarial valuations and separately for Company accounts, statements will be made regarding levels of solvency (percentages) and sterling values of surplus or deficit.

Broadly, these may be described as valuations on an ongoing basis and a discontinuance basis but with the latter qualified that it will not actually apply if a scheme is discontinued as the cost will be whatever it will be to buy out benefits.

Actuaries and Auditors should be asked to explain very simply and clearly what the different figures mean and in what circumstances they apply.

71. Manage the conflicts, the difficult and the contentious

The actuarial valuation and funding assessment processes crystallise a number of things and require reliable data, investment and accounting records.

A reliable process for information gathering and delivery to the correct people on time should not cause conflict provided there is agreement on what is needed and why and by whom and when.

Working to the same facts then allows the more difficult and contentious to be addressed in a balanced manner.

15. CONTROLLING, CONTROLS AND UNDER CONTROL

72. Beware the autocrats and ditherers

Intuitive and decisive individuals or groups are refreshing if they are sufficiently on top of the subject and aware of the implications and potential consequences.

'Control freaks', (who may themselves be out of control) can be very disruptive if issuing impulsive commands that are impossible to achieve.

At the other end of the spectrum are those who expect endless streams of information and detail with no clear reason why and provide no clear outcome as a consequence. These undesirable traits can be reduced by ensuring that sensible internal control procedures are in place and operated.

A miscellany of responses to the same question:

"!!!!****do as I say"

"um.....do what you think best"

"Give me a report on it. I don't need all the detail but I expect John will"

"Do what we always do"

"Ask the lawyers"

"I can't remember, but didn't I tell you before?"

"Do we really have to go over the same thing time and time again?"

73. Strive for consistency and balance

Exceptional situations will occur and changes will be required.

Continually changing requirements that are often never quite understood add to confusion and problems.

Stable and logical control procedures that are well understood stand a better chance of identifying risks and problems before they become severe.

74. Ponder this question: What is the difference between an internal and external control?

In a pensions context this is quite difficult as so many different permutations could apply as to how pensions are managed.

A straightforward example of a control procedure is a bank mandate – who is allowed to sign cheques

15. CONTROLLING, CONTROLS AND UNDER CONTROL (CONTINUED)

A CAMEO

Ventriloquist:
"Help me.....I'm being taken over by my gummy"

Dummy:
"Great....Now I can get a decent Bottle of Beer"

"Be clear who is pulling the strings"

or authorise payments? It is rarely advisable to give one person sole authority but in smaller schemes it may well be appropriate for a trustee to authorise all payments.

Alternatively, the smallness itself may be the reason for wanting this sub contracted to an external party. If so, are payments from a third party bank account or is the third party authorised to operate the trustee account?

The boundaries become blurred and there are doubts then about who is bearing the risk of fraud etc.

The practical way round this, therefore is to ignore the words' internal' and 'external' and ensure control procedures are in place across the whole.

As a consequence be aware of and record your Agent's control procedures. Question your Agents on their operating procedures and be satisfied that they are robust.

75. Know and be confident that it is under control

Things can go wrong and will. Perfection is impossible to define and consequently impossible to achieve.

The closer to perfection, the more visible the tiniest flaw becomes, so things must be kept in proportion.

The solution therefore is not to get everybody rushing about in all directions checking up on everybody else, but to have a structure and reporting procedures in place to be able to provide assurances to all parties that the significant and important matters are under control.

16. COMPLIANCE AND GOVERNANCE, RECORDS AND MEETINGS

76. Comply and demonstrate compliance

Put bluntly, you have no choice in some matters. Laws have to be obeyed, however incomprehensible, unfair or illogical.

Codes of practice are less binding but, nonetheless, there is an expectation that they should be followed.

Similarly, there is little point in having your own defined procedures and policies if these are not adhered to.

Having no procedures or policies is **not** a viable alternative.

A dictionary says:

“**Compliance**:*n:* acting in accordance with request or command etc.”

“**Governance**:*n*:act or manner or function of governing.”

“**Good**:*n:* having right qualities, adequate, proper, virtuous, morally excellent, worthy, well-behaved, agreeable, suitable, considerable, valid.”

77. Identify the ‘must do’ changes

Draw a distinction between knowing what you have to tackle and knowing how to tackle it. The latter can take the time and easily run out of control. So can the former if there is no clear mechanism to identify the law changes and regulations that need to be complied with and the effective dates.

Draw a clear distinction between what **may** happen in the future and what **must** happen.

Bear in mind that pensions can be influenced by various aspects of law, e.g. age discrimination, sex discrimination, human rights and finance, as well as pensions legislation itself.

Once you know what you have to tackle, it is easier then to prioritise and implement in a controlled fashion.

16. COMPLIANCE AND GOVERNANCE, RECORDS AND MEETINGS (CONTINUED)

78. Don't forget existing obligations to comply

Set up regular routines. There are many obligations when identified that are capable of fitting into regular routines.

The following few examples, covering various disciplines but all having pension implications, should be incorporated in clear timetables that can be easily checked against: annual pensions increases; Regulator return, PPF levy, tax payments and returns, annual accounts, actuarial valuations, contribution deadlines, insurance renewals.

79. Comply with requests appropriately

'Appropriate' is a frequently used word in various codes of practice. It is an ill defined word and therefore requires the exercise of judgement.

All requests, therefore, cannot be complied with, but efficient and timely acknowledgements and responses can prevent matters getting out of hand – no-one likes being ignored or left in a continuing state of uncertainty.

80. Operate 'good' governance

Looking at the range covered by the dictionary definitions of 'good', there is no absolute.

You clearly don't want to act in a 'bad' manner; you (plural, i.e. all people involved) need to 'govern' your own responsibilities in a 'good' manner.

You may wish to make it 'better' and aspire to 'best practice' but the aim of 'good' is not ambiguous in a common sense way.

Whilst complaints and disputes may well provide evidence that all is not well, silence or vacuums in communication, reports, documents and records are also indicators that good practice is potentially vulnerable.

81. Have efficiently run meetings and sensible methodologies for records, document retention and reference

These bring everything together in a co-ordinated way.

Inefficiently run or poorly prepared meetings are a major source of unnecessary cost. Not only in terms of company Executive time, but in terms of Agents time which is often chargeable at premium rates.

17. RISKS AND PROTECTION

A famous safety slogan:
"Stop, Look and listen"

Take your pick of the proverbs:
"look before you leap"
"A stitch in time"
"Fools rush in where wise men fear to tread"

A wolf once said:
"I'll huff and I'll puff and I'll blow your house down"

82. Accept that risks are inevitable

There is no such thing as risk free. Manage risk sensibly and proportionately.

83. Work from the top

The top level risks e.g. failure of the employer to be able to support itself or the scheme or a substantial funding shortfall with no means of remedy have the last resort protection of the Pension Protection Fund (PPF).

Although a comforting protection and possibly a convenient escape route, it should not be an objective to enter the PPF.

Be aware that the buying out of benefits could move protection away from the PPF to the financial services environment.

84. Revisit the Key 3

No apologies for emphasising Administration, Funding and Investment and the need to minimize risks in these areas.

Absolute insurance is not available, so the major risks need identifying, assessing and any potential loopholes or sloppiness controlled and minimised.

Don't overlook the basic regulations like data protection and anti money-laundering or common sense procedures for data security, back-up and recovery, fraud prevention etc.

Insurance/Assurance may also be a specific remedy for sharing or sub-contracting a risk such as benefits to be paid out on death. Each of the topics will have its own sub elements of risk to be assessed and controlled.

85. Manage the 'science' of imprecision and conjecture

General Economic projections, Business projections, Investment projections and Funding assumptions and projections all have major impact on pension judgements and decisions.

The adoption of a safe or cautious view by one party can create a serious risk for another.

However far apart, serious efforts must be made to recognise the full range of risks; some of the most contentious areas require acknowledgement that compromise may be necessary to find a resolution.

86. Act sensibly for reputational or liability protection

Certain protections may feature in the Trust Documentation to limit liability or responsibility.

Insurances such as Trustee, Directors and Employers Liability should be suitably put in place. Trustees should not rely on Directors and Officers cover alone. Understand the impact of exclusions as many may undermine the real value of protection.

When ceasing to be a Trustee, ensure there is adequate run off cover. But note none of these will, or should be expected to deal with acts of criminality or fraud.

A VARIATION ON A THEME:

"What is half full to one is half empty to another; the difference can be enormous. The former is full of optimism, anticipation, and faith that the additional half will soon be added and the full potential reached. The latter is sadly nostalgic, reflecting on past enjoyment and clinging possessively to the remainder. The distinction becomes less obvious and any enjoyment fades if both remaining halves are left stale or stagnant."

17. RISKS AND PROTECTION (CONTINUED)

Take appropriate advice, but maintain a sense of proportion when assessing the extent of advice required. Acting with good will and in good faith should help protect reputations.

Acting against strong advice is a risk. Advisers should give sound and helpful advice but should refrain from giving absolute hard-nosed advice that gives no room for manoeuvre in difficult situations, unless there really is no option otherwise.

87. Meet the deadlines

Timing can be of great significance, for example badly timed investment decisions or their practical implementation.

Other processes may have absolute deadlines like paying pensions on a due date or paying tax or submitting a Regulator return.

Avoid the risk of fines, complaints etc by being on top of deadlines.

88. Identify what others have in place

It is prudent to check what Insurances and indemnities are in place for those you are employing as agents.

18. CHANGES AND CHALLENGES

89. Be prepared

Continuity and stability form the foundations.

The Pensions Regulator has requirements to be notified of certain things and there are obligations falling on various parties to report breaches.

Whether driven internally or a reaction to external influences, dealing with changes and problems requires awareness and ready access to the right information and people.

Remember that significant events may well require to be notified to the Pensions Regulator. Or clearance obtained before action is allowed to be taken, with different responsibilities falling to the Employer and Trustees depending upon whether it is deemed to be Scheme related or Employer related.

Examples of the Regulator's Notifiable Events are:
Payment of benefits on favourable terms;
Employer trading wrongfully;
Conviction of senior personnel;
Decision not to pay debt to scheme;
Decision to cease business in the UK.

Check out the requirements when dealing with significant events or proposed changes.

A VARIATION ON A THEME:

"The Statement
'A change is as good as a rest' is too hard to contemplate for the lazy man. The rest may challenge the truth of it. The lazy will selfishly strive to make changes as restfully as possible for themselves and themselves alone. The thoughtful will strive to make changes as restfully as possible for all concerned to keep them alert for their next change."

19. THE FULL PICTURE

90. Pull it together and pull together
91. Keep clear records of what is known
92. Plan as much as you can
93. Be prepared for the unpredictable
94. Keep thinking about the possible
95. Do the essential
96. Manage conflicts calmly and sensibly
97. Use resources proportionately and appropriately
98. Keep an open mind
99. Manage and deal with others efficiently
100. Make time your friend
101. Avoid people being boxed into corners
102. Communicate well at all levels
103. Manage documents and records efficiently
104. Keep reviewing but don't disrupt
105. Build as much as possible into routine
106. Apply common sense
107. Reduce reliance on memory
108. Establish structures to reassure all involved that all is under control

20. AND FINALLY

½ Don't forget...

You plan to manage and control the Beastie;
it should not be controlling you.

"....it's a matter of trust"

NOTES AREA

NOTES AREA

APPENDIX 1

The Pensions Regulator's first six years and future plans

The Pensions Act 2004 established the Pensions Regulator (TPR) as the Regulatory Authority in the UK for work-based pensions replacing the Occupational Pensions Regulatory Authority (OPRA) on 6 April 2005.

Part 1, Section 5 (1) of the Act described the Pensions Regulator objectives as follows:

"The main objectives of the Regulator in exercising its functions are -

a. To protect the benefits under occupational pension schemes of, or in respect of, members of such schemes,
b. To protect the benefits under personal pension schemes of, or in respect of, members of such schemes ,
c. To reduce the risk of situations arising which may lead to compensation being payable from the Pensions Protection Fund, and
d. To promote, and improve understanding of, the good administration of work-based pension schemes."

David Norgrove was appointed in January 2005 as the first Chairman of the Pensions Regulator, and his 6 years tenure has now been completed (Jan 2011). As has been highlighted by the introduction to this book the last 6 years have seen dramatic changes to the pensions landscape, brought about by unprecedented circumstances. Navigating a safe passage over this period has been extraordinarily difficult for the majority of Companies managing defined benefit pension schemes.

It has also been a challenge for the Regulator. David Norgrove made his last speech as Chairman to the National Association of Pension Funds Trustee Conference in December 2010. The Pensions Regulator has kindly granted permission for the full text to be reproduced in this book. The speech is a succinct summary of many of the key issues facing the management of work-based pensions and also throws light on the Regulators objectives in the coming years.

NAPF annual trustee conference

David Norgrove, chair, speaking at the NAPF annual trustee conference December 2010

Introduction

I would like to thank the NAPF for inviting me here today for what will be my last speech as chair of The Pensions Regulator. As some of you will know I step down at the end of the month after six years in the chair.

I've found the job endlessly interesting and challenging, mixing as it does finance, business, social policy, politics and of course governance of the Regulator itself. One of my first jobs as chair was to work with Tony Hobman to get the operational side of the regulator up-and-running to deal with scheme funding, risk and avoidance. It meant changes in people, changes in culture and the learning of new skills for staff who moved over from OPRA. We also put in place a large secondment programme with banks, law firms accountants and actuaries so that we could both learn about current practice and teach about our approach.

Thanks usually come at the end of a speech but I want to start by paying a warm tribute to all the staff at the Regulator, to all the Directors, including particularly to two, June Mulroy and Stuart Weatherley who have been there almost from the start, and to Bill Galvin and Tony Hobman, my two CEOs. I have been fortunate to work with such committed and able people.

The shock of the recent economic downturn meant that we all had to learn to run almost as soon as we could walk, and we are now operating an unprecedented caseload.

Things have got increasingly busy. A number of high profile cases have come to a head; cases which have seen us use the strongest of our powers.

These cases, as well as reaching the end of the first full cycle of triennial valuations have taught us important lessons about the way the industry has chosen to interact with us and our DB framework in particular. I'll talk more about both of these in a moment or two.

The continued decline in open DB provision over the past few years has seen a sharp turn of focus towards DC and the challenges it poses to schemes and to members. This includes us and I will share with you today some of our early thinking about regulating DC in the future.

Finally, it would be wrong to look at the pensions industry today without considering the impact of workplace pensions reform and the role we will play in effecting change and helping many more members save for their retirement.

But before we look too far ahead, let me take a few minutes to look back at the lessons we have learnt from our work over the past 6 years.

DB funding and the shifting pensions landscape

The Pensions Regulator was set up under the Pensions Act 2004, in the wake of a spate of pension scheme collapses that saw around 150,000 people lose some of their pension. It was clear to all that a new regulatory framework, with a greater focus on risks to members was required.

Scheme Specific Funding was introduced, and with it came a new vocabulary, with terms such as 'recovery plans', 'technical provisions' and 'employer covenant'.

We've seen many of those first schemes again, as they undertake their second round of valuations since the move to Scheme Specific Funding. And what we've seen over the last few years is a marked improvement in the standards of work by everyone associated with DB schemes even when set against a backdrop of worsening and uncertain economic conditions.

The economic crisis has meant that pension schemes and sponsoring employers have experienced three of the toughest years in living memory. There is no doubt that without proper funding plans in place the impact of the recession would have been even greater. Without them we could have faced real problems in future years and the PPF would potentially have come under significant pressure.

The downturn was a major test for the new regulatory framework. On the whole, I believe it has proved resilient in protecting members and the PPF, while allowing trustees and sponsors a reasonable amount of flexibility to manage liabilities in line with our view that a desirable outcome for the scheme is usually provided by security from a solvent employer. The use of contingent assets is up 16% in the past year or so, according to the recently published TPR/PPF 'Purple Book'. Similarly, the unweighted average recovery plan length has increased by one year to 9.4 years, according to the most recent data, and - despite the financial pressure on companies - total employer deficit reduction contributions during 2009-10 were up £2.6bn to £29.1bn.

There have also been major improvements in the key areas of administration and governance. The Trustee Knowledge and Understanding code set benchmarks for trustees and the Trustee toolkit today provides learning support for over 30,000 users. New tools and resources have also sprung up in response to emerging issues and challenges facing trustees, issues like buy-outs and buy-ins and assessing the employer covenant. Again our work on the core issues like data collecting and management have had a material impact on schemes, evidenced by a reduction in wind-up periods.

But there is no room for complacency. Schemes are only marginally better funded then when the scheme specific funding regime was introduced five years ago. Despite everyone's best efforts, the economic conditions have largely counteracted the gains that schemes had started to make before the downturn. Contributions have had to run to keep up with rising longevity, falling discount rates and shortfalls in expected investment returns.

We clearly can't have a situation where we move from recovery plan to recovery plan and don't get any nearer their end. As conditions improve we expect schemes to once again narrow the gap between assets and liabilities as they did in 2006 and 2007.

Closed schemes

That brings me to a more general point.

In 2005 there were widespread predictions of the end of DB. Five years on good DB provision does remain and these predictions have not been entirely borne out.

However, the market is certainly in transition – many schemes are now closed to new members, 58 per cent in 2010 compared to 44 per cent four years ago. And an increasing number are closed to future accrual, 21% in 2010 up from 12 per cent four years ago.

We are in the end game for these schemes and this has a range of implications.

It means that sponsoring employers will have an even greater incentive to de-risk and to shift the scheme off balance sheet if at all possible. I see it as one of the achievements of the regulator in the past six years that we were able to stop in their tracks those businesses that proposed to take schemes off a sponsor's hands for an amount short of buy out. We have seen enough during this recession that those business models may well have been a disaster for members and the PPF.

But there will be further challenges, requiring alertness on the part of the regulator, trustees and advisers.

If I was asked to make predictions about the longer term, my view is that scheme governance, funding expectations and de-risking will be amongst the key challenges for the increasing number of closed DB schemes.

As schemes close and mature in age profile, over time a smaller proportion will have close ties with the employer. And with fewer current staff involved in a DB scheme, the employer's interest in the day-to-day running will also lessen. There is also likely to be pressure from shareholders to reduce the sponsor's exposure to risk.

As a means of tackling these challenges, there will be a need to ensure that the governance model is robust to cope with an ageing membership and the ever widening distance from the scheme sponsor. In my personal view, I believe too that standards of funding will need to continue to rise and that indeed they will do so. Where schemes have not yet achieved funding at 100 per cent of their technical provisions we should ensure that they certainly never fall below the funding required to cover at least PPF benefit levels. We should be less inclined to accept funding of below PPF benefit levels under any circumstances. Where funding goes to in the future, will depend on how much protection government and business agree to give. But we need to bear in mind that these liabilities will be on company balance sheets for decades to come. It may well be in the interests of business to get these legacy liabilities out of their hair and the trustees off their backs, by funding to self sufficiency in the longer term and de-risking to take away the volatility. These are major questions that will be a matter for my successor and no doubt for vigorous debate.

Schemes where liabilities are likely never to be met

Over the past year or so we have highlighted the role of the employer in underwriting the liabilities of the scheme and the impact of this covenant on the funding decisions trustees make.

Where the covenant is strong, it provides trustees with some flexibility in how they meet the scheme's liabilities. But where it is weak, the opposite is true.

There are a small number of schemes where the liabilities are never likely to be met by the sponsors.

The employer covenant in a handful of cases is so weak that even allowing for this support, these schemes are by any measure insolvent. They can only hope to meet their promises by taking very high levels of investment risk with significant potential to go wrong.

For such schemes we believe the starting point has to be that any deficit should not be allowed to increase. There are two aspects to this.

First is the accrual of benefits. Where an employer is unlikely to ever get close to providing funding for benefits already accrued, it is common sense that they should look seriously at whether future accrual should continue.

Secondly, as set out in our covenant guidance, investment risk should only be taken to the extent that it can be underwritten by the employer.

It's not right for schemes to take excessive investment risks to bridge the funding gap where there is a fragile employer. This is essentially gambling with other people's money.

If the strategy back-fires, leaving the scheme in a worse position, a minority of younger members will carry the strain and PPF levy payers may have to meet the shortfall.

The Ilford judgement makes it very clear that trustees cannot rely upon the existence of the PPF safety net as part of their strategy for improving the scheme's funding.

We have already encountered a very small number of schemes in this difficult position and we are exploring the various ways open to us to deal with this situation.

Such schemes raise a new and challenging set of circumstances for us to work through with trustees and with the sponsoring employers and we intend to say more next year.

As is already the case, we will not hesitate to use our powers in situations where a weak covenant has been 'manufactured' in a bid to offload the scheme.

There are two other matters I want to discuss before I turn to DC. They are enhanced transfer values and the use of our powers.

Enhanced transfer values

This time last year I raised concerns with regard to enhanced transfer values (ETVs), and - following consultation on our revised guidance back in July - we will be publishing the final guidance later this week.

It is fair to say there has been a lively debate in the industry. Whilst I know I will struggle to convince some of you today, I feel it's important to make a few points about this vital issue.

Firstly in my personal opinion it's ironic that some in the industry have said that Government and TPR should do more to maintain DB provision while baulking at any suggestion that members should think twice about transferring out of a DB scheme.

We are not saying that transfers will always be inappropriate. We are though still asking trustees to begin from the presumption that these exercises are not in most members' best interests, and that is based on our belief that in the overwhelming majority of situations this will indeed be the case. However we do recognise that there will be individual and specific circumstances in which a transfer may be in the member's best interests.

We point to these in our final guidance, to be published later this week. They are where a members' life expectancy is limited; where no dependants will be supported long term by the DB pension; where the member is a sophisticated investor and is specifically looking to balance the risks in a portfolio of retirement benefits; or where the level of benefit is significantly higher than the PPF cap and as such would be cut if the schemes entered the PPF. And even in these cases, trustees need to be satisfied that allowing the member in question to transfer is in the interests of the remaining members of the scheme.

The number of members falling into this category will likely be a small proportion of all those offered a transfer.

Our concern is that members – who are essentially in the same position as consumers in these transactions – may not get the protection they need to make the best decision. We would be failing in our objective to protect members if we turned a blind eye.

And why do we believe members need protection? Well, we have seen some concerning behaviour, for example where the member is offered advice paid for by the employer but on the condition that members take that advice. We have also seen examples where excessive pressure is placed on members to make a decision, with daily phone calls, emails and even home visits.

It is also a simple fact that it's very difficult for members to gauge whether giving up a DB pension promise – in exchange for a cash transfer into a DC scheme – will be in their best interests over the long term.

Offers that involve cash incentives are likely to result in less objective decision-making, and members may struggle to evaluate the strength of the offer in the context of the benefits they are giving up and the risks that are being transferred to them. They need to be able to make an informed choice, and take such decisions with their eyes open.

Trustees can help to safeguard members by ensuring that any such exercises are well-run, with members' interests at the forefront. Our approach is consistent with the FSA's approach to contract-based pensions and we published a joint statement with them in July. Whether carrying out transfer exercise is the right choice or not, is not for us to judge. However, if a sponsor does decide to carry out a transfer exercise we will expect it to be fair and that members will be made aware of the risk they are taking on.

Given the gravity of the decision, the difficult financial equation, and potential for detriment if they get the decision wrong, we believe our stance is reasonable and proportionate.

Use of the regulator's powers

In 2010 the regulator continues to use its powers in the most effective way we know how – as a deterrent. By expending a significant amount of effort on education and enablement, we can minimise the need to enforce at a later stage.

We do not use our powers if we can avoid it. But over the past five years there have been many occasions where it has been necessary. Since 2005 we have requested, and been granted by the Determinations Panel, the power to remove 14 individual trustees from schemes and to appoint 25 trustees to schemes. In the past two years alone we have used the power to request information from employers, advisers or schemes on 88 occasions. And on five separate occasions we have been granted to power to raid properties and to retain any documents which may help with our investigations. So we don't sit on our hands.

Sometimes we reach the brink of exercising our heavier powers. Just a couple of months ago we were poised to use the power to set technical provisions and impose a recovery plan for the first time, in respect of the EMI pension scheme. This had been a long case and we welcomed the fact that the trustees and employer were eventually able to come to an agreement which was reasonable for all the parties involved.

This was a high-profile case that received media attention. Most of the time we are in the situation of having helped to deliver a positive outcome without being able to tell anyone about it. Legislation – designed to protect employer' commercial confidentiality and encourage people to share information with us - rightly places restrictions on what we can and cannot say publicly about our interventions, with most case-specific information falling into the latter category.

When we do release details of our interventions, as we have this year, it demonstrates that the regulator is not just all bark. It can bite. But we would prefer not to have to use our heavier powers at all. The regulator's Determinations Panel provides a crucial, impartial, check on the way in which we exercise these powers.

Some recent cases are also testing the scope of our powers. I should emphasise that we don't see this as a negative exercise. It is important for us to have clarity around their reach.

DC and The Pensions Regulator's plans

I now turn to DC, which has gained increasing attention over the past few years. And this will only increase as membership grows and as we approach auto-enrolment from 2012.

We have a duty to protect the benefits of all members and we must therefore ensure that DC scheme members are offered the appropriate protection and support they need to make good choices about their savings. They also have the right, just like their DB counterparts, to be in a well run, high quality, good value scheme.

While there are many excellent DC schemes, members face risks including the consequences of poor administration, high charges, inadequate contributions, inappropriate investment choices and insufficient or sub standard communication.

Members in each different type of scheme face risks to varying degrees. For example members in small trust-based schemes may be certain that the trustees should be acting in their interest. However the risk of insufficient resource and knowledge within the board means they may be at higher risk of poor administration than those in for example a large GPP where the provider has greater resource to expend on each member.

We don't make a judgement on which type of provision is best, but we do recognise that the different segments may call for somewhat different regulatory approaches.

Knowing what approach is best comes down at least in part to knowing who is accountable for the decisions that lead to members receiving adequate retirement income.

- How much can we rely on the member to make good choices?
- What can and should the employer do to ensure that provision is appropriate for their staff? and
- What is the role of the provider and the trustee?

In trust-based DC schemes the accountability is clear. There is less clarity in DC contract-based schemes. We have been liaising with our colleagues at DWP, the FSA and Treasury, as well as with major players within the pensions industry, to explore what a safe, secure and sustainable DC market might look like.

In the New Year, we plan to consult with the industry on our thoughts in this area, with the aim of publishing a revised DC regulatory framework in late 2011.

The future

Looking ahead, The Pensions Regulator will play a key role in delivering some of the most significant and far reaching changes in generations to the pension system.

In another six years time, all existing employers will have reached their auto-enrolment duty date and up to 8 million people will have been auto-enrolled into a qualifying pension scheme, helping to reduce the number of people – currently over 7 million – who are not saving enough for their retirement.

Following the completion of the 'Making Auto-enrolment work' review back in October, our work is now flat out - developing the process for registration and maximising employer compliance while minimising unnecessary regulatory burdens. We are mindful of the impact on all employers, but particularly small and micro-employers, which are less likely to be engaged in pensions already. To help employers to get ready we will communicate directly with all employers at least 12 months before their duty date and then again three months before.

This communication is so important because it will take time for employers to get ready for auto-enrolment, to update payroll and HR systems, and to communicate the changes with their employees. This time is crucial for employers, many of whom up until now may have had little or no interaction with pensions, to become familiar with their new duties.

We will do everything we can to educate and enable employers to fulfil their duties. During 2011 we will be publishing guidance for employers and trustees, and their advisers, explaining the new duties in as much detail as is possible. There will also be interactive tools designed specifically for small and micro-employers. These will ask a number of questions of the employer and in response deliver the relevant information for that employer's situation.

We want to see maximum compliance and we will do everything we can to help employers fulfil their duties. As in all our work so far we do not want to hand out penalties where this can be avoided. No penalty will be issued without due warning and the opportunity for the employer to rectify the situation. We cannot of course leave deliberate non-compliance unchecked and we will have powers to deal with this behaviour.

Our strategy for enforcement will be published for consultation in 2011 and we will look for feedback from across the industry and from employers.

Conclusion

It has been a fascinating six years. When I took the job friends thought I was mad. Some thought it would be boring. The more informed thought it was not doable and that my doom was inevitable. We were bound to fail. I do not believe that we have failed. I began by thanking the staff at the Regulator for their part in that. I now want to thank the NAPF and above all you the trustees for the part you play. Without you we would certainly fail.

Thank you.

Web site link <http://www.thepensionsregulator.gov.uk/doc-library/david-norgrove-napf-annual-trustee-conference-speech.aspx>

APPENDIX 2

TIPS Listing Summary

A Common Purpose

Having set up pension arrangements, making sure the objectives are still clear

1. **Ask those you are dealing with if they agree with the first statement**
2. **Concentrate on the important**
3. **Identify and work to the priorities**
4. **Clarify and agree the policies and principles before tackling the detail**
5. **Involve the right people at the right time**
6. **Distinguish between objectives, facts, opinions, interpretations and judgements**

The Pension Schemes and the voids

Looking at the specific schemes and identifying the gaps and avoiding the voids

7. **Consider whose problem this is**
8. **Start by defining what you know**
9. **Locate and keep permanently accessible the legal documents establishing the scheme**
10. **Research and record the origins and background**
11. **Keep your Trust Deed and Rules up to date**
12. **Falling between stools: Think "Void"**

Powers, Responsibilities, Decisions and Delegation

Being clear who is allowed to do what

13. **Make sure those involved work within their powers**
14. **Summarise the powers and make this summary easily available**
15. **Make sure decisions are agreed by a correctly constituted quorum**
16. **Delegate appropriately**
17. **Understand the powers to appoint agents and apply these powers correctly**
18. **Take advice appropriately but avoid the tail wagging the dog**

Customers

Accepting that all aspects are linked and all parties need to serve as well as be served

19. **Ensure all parties accept the need to serve**
20. **Serve as you would like to be served**

Employers

Assessing the Employers involvement

21. Identify the role of the Employer

22. Understand the Organisational Structure of the Employer

23. Understand the people

24. Structure to suit the Organisation

25. Beware of incompatible practices

26. Consider pensions as soon as possible in business changes

Trustees

Considering how the trustees operate

27. Be clear of the trustee constitution and methodology of appointment

28. Specify expectations and special roles

29. Plan timetables, routines and Meetings

30. Deserve the Trust

Agents

Understanding the appointment and roles of Agents

31. Appoint external agents sensibly

32. Keep agents under control

33. Make changes logically and justifiably

34. Remember that experts in their specialist areas are not automatically experts on your scheme and its circumstances

Knowledge and Understanding

Considering training at all levels and what needs to be understood

35. Aim for continuity and combined knowledge

36. Distinguish between functionality and decision making

37. Acknowledge the knowledge gaps

Benefit design

Reviewing the promises, guarantees and discretions

38. Make guarantees the priority

39. Be clear about the discretions, practices and other potential obligations

40. Take major changes very seriously

Finances

Flagging up the various layers of finance

41. Unravel the layers of cost

42. Be clear who is commissioning work, who should pay and the mechanics of authorising and paying invoices

43. Plan

44. Ensure effective practices

45. Have clear Accounting practices and procedures

Three Key Topics

Pondering the relative importance of Administration, Funding and Investment

46. Stand back and think of the big picture

Administration

Addressing what is meant by administration and considering some of the components

47. Try to define what is meant by Administration for your scheme

48. Concentrate on the functionality

49. Don't ignore the need for the overview

50. Have an open discussion about data reliability

51. Receive reports and identify the weak links and weaknesses

52. Don't forget member communication, time limits and complaints procedures

53. Adopt a timetable approach for other elements of administration

Investment

Considering strategies structures and practices

54. Understand the investment extremes and what options are in the middle

55. Understand the types and styles of investment management approach

56. Understand the support needs

57. Consider the strategy in the right order

58. Identify the Cash-flow impact

59. Identify acceptable levels of complexity

60. Set the right benchmarks, monitor appropriately and understand the costs

61. Review regularly and manage changes sensibly

62. Spare a thought for the members

Funding

Understanding the different perspectives and streamlining the process

63. Dream a dream (some might say now the impossible dream)
64. Don't panic about the Nightmare
65. Understand the Actuary's position
66. Understand the Employers' position
67. Understand the Trustees' position
68. Find the common ground
69. Understand the Pension Regulators position
70. Understand what is meant by surplus or deficit
71. Manage the conflicts, the difficult and the contentious

Controlling, controls and under control

Assessing the implications of various elements of control

72. Beware the autocrats and ditherers
73. Strive for consistency and balance
74. Ponder this question: What is the difference between an internal and external control?
75. Know and be confident that it is under control

Compliance and Governance, Records and Meetings

Weighing up the needs to comply and ensure all aspects are sensibly governed

76. Comply and demonstrate compliance
77. Identify the 'must do' changes
78. Don't forget existing obligations to comply
79. Comply with requests appropriately
80. Operate 'good' governance
81. Have efficiently run meetings and sensible methodologies for records, document retention and reference

Risks and Protection

Contemplating potential areas of risk, precautions and insurances

82. Accept that risks are inevitable
83. Work from the top
84. Revisit the Key 3
85. Manage the 'science' of imprecision and conjecture

86. Act sensibly for reputational or liability protection
87. Meet the deadlines
88. Identify what others have in place

Changes and challenges

Acknowledging there will be changes and preparing

89. Be prepared

The full picture

Pulling the threads together

90. Pull it together and pull together
91. Keep clear records of what is known
92. Plan as much as you can
93. Be prepared for the unpredictable
94. Keep thinking about the possible
95. Do the essential
96. Manage conflicts calmly and sensibly
97. Use resources proportionately and appropriately
98. Keep an open mind
99. Manage and deal with others efficiently
100. Make time your friend
101. Avoid people being boxed into corners
102. Communicate well at all levels
103. Manage documents and records efficiently
104. Keep reviewing but don't disrupt
105. Build as much as possible into routine
106. Apply common sense
107. Reduce reliance on memory
108. Establish structures to reassure all involved that all is under control

AND FINALLY

½ Don't forget…. ".... it's a matter of trust"